new orleans' favorite shotguns

by Mary Fitzpatrick and Alex Lemann

underwritten through the generosity of the
Eugenie and Joseph Jones Family Foundation

published by the Preservation Resource Center of New Orleans

First published in the United States of America in 2007 by

PRESERVATION RESOURCE CENTER OF NEW ORLEANS
923 Tchoupitoulas Street
New Orleans, Louisiana 70130
504/ 581-7032
www.prcno.org

© 2007 Preservation Resource Center of New Orleans
Designer: Paula Coughlin, Typosition
Proofreader: Sarah Bonnette
Literary Sales Manager: Averil Oberhelman, aoberhelman@prcno.org, 504.581.7032 www.prcno.org

Preservation Resource Center of New Orleans is a registered IRS 501 (c) (3) non-profit organization. Since 1974, the PRC's mission has been to promote the preservation, restoration and revitalization of New Orleans' historic neighborhoods and architecture.

Printed in China.
ISBN 978-0-9773165-1-9

Front cover photo: Fences Sky, by J. Stirling Barrett

contents

New Orleans
Neighborhoods in
National Register of Historic Places

GENTILLY TERRACE

SOUTH LAKEVIEW

CITY PARK

METAIRIE ROAD

CITY PARK AVENUE

PARKVIEW

ESPLANADE RIDGE

NEW MARIGNY

ORLEANS

Lower Ninth Ward

CANAL

AIRLINE DRIVE

MID-CITY

SOUTH BROAD

TREMÉ

FRENCH QUARTER

FAUBOURG MARIGNY

BYWATER

HOLY CROSS

TULANE

EARHART EXPRESSWAY

CENTRAL BUSINESS DISTRICT

ALGIERS POINT

BROADMOOR

CLAIBORNE

CARROLLTON

UPTOWN

NAPOLEON

CENTRAL CITY

LOWER GARDEN DISTRICT

GARDEN DISTRICT

ST. CHARLES

AUDUBON PARK

MAGAZINE

IRISH CHANNEL

TCHOUPITOULAS

MISSISSIPPI RIVER

WEST BANK

introduction

A group calling itself "Friends of the Shotgun House" moved the last intact shotgun in Santa Monica to the airport parking lot in order to save it from demolition. The members are now raising money to relocate and renovate this lone relic from the late 19th-century building boom in Southern California.

ROBERT J. CANGELOSI, JR.

Unimaginable. In New Orleans, with an estimated 25,000 shotguns in the National Register districts alone, this simple and straightforward shelter is still the house that all Orleanians have in common, as emblematic of the city as bungalows are to Chicago, yurts to Central Asia and rowhouses to Baltimore.

First built in New Orleans as a worker's cottage, the shotgun has retained its modest roots for 175 years, while at the same time adding hallways, camelbacks and great rooms. It's been gussied up with Italianate facades, stripped down to the cypress boards and industrialized with concrete countertops and wire banisters. Fixed up in one neighborhood and frozen in time just a few blocks away, this narrow

6

house – with its row of rooms one after the other, raised foundation, louvered shutters and high ceilings – complies with ease to the taste and budget of each owner.

Shotguns have served as a compact starter home for newlyweds Anne and Will Summerour, a spacious place for Ellen and Mac Ball to rear their family, part of a complex of shops for retailers Bee Fitzpatrick and Dabney Jacob, a restaurant for Leah Chase and a lifelong residence for 90-year-old Mildred Bennett. These homes are the common architectural thread of young and old, rich and poor, and every ethnic group that has settled in New Orleans.

In the early 20th century, jazz pulsated from shotgun parlors out to the street, where funeral processions and start-up spasm bands were part of life. Great characters, real and imaginary, came out of these houses. "Can you imagine Ignatius J. Reilly living anywhere but in a shotgun?" architect Rob Stumm asks, referring to the Pulitzer Prize-winning classic *A Confederacy of Dunces*.

Historically, with one room leading into the next and little privacy, the shotgun obliged families to be close and neighborhoods to be tightly knit. Aunts and uncles, grandparents, and grown brothers and sisters commonly lived – and still do – on either side of a shotgun "double," as in double-barrel. Five generations of Robert Smith's family live in two adjacent shotgun houses on Dauphine St. in Holy Cross, and that's the pattern in many neighborhoods.

MARY FITZPATRICK

Often, families outgrew the few bedrooms in a shotgun, so children slept in a corner of the living room or in the dining room on a cot, which had to be removed for the traditional Sunday dinner when even more family members came together after Mass. "Get up, you lazy sinner. We need the sheets for tablecloths, it's almost time for dinner," was a good-humored jab at a child sleeping next to the Frigidaire in the dining room.

Stoops and porches compensated for the tight quarters. While children played in the street, moms cast a net of informants across the neighborhood. "In those days, all the neighbors raised each others' children," says 88-year-old Marie Jolissaint Durette, speaking about the Esplanade Ridge neighborhood where she has lived her entire life. "If I was sitting on my stoop and chastised your child, you accepted it. If a neighbor lady heard my son Kenny was up to trouble, she'd call me right away. I didn't have to leave my house to know exactly what my children were up to."

Densely packed rows of shotguns have shaped the communal culture of generations in New Orleans, regardless of income or color. Unfortunately, after Hurricane Katrina and the ensuing levee failures in 2005, thousands of these houses – built of old-growth swamp cypress and designed to flood, drain and dry – were destroyed by rushing water, demolished by wrecking crews or abandoned by owners and tenants. The loss of so many shotgun homes is both an architectural and a cultural tragedy.

It is inconceivable that New Orleans would ever spawn a sister group to Santa Monica's

AVERIL OBERHELMAN

519 State St., Uptown, Drew Lang, architect

Friends of The One and Only Shotgun House. However, in a city that since Katrina needs all the friends it can get, we can certainly preserve and celebrate the 25,000 we have.

Mary Fitzpatrick

The last shotgun in Santa Monica. shotgunhouse.org

spectacular vernacular

AVERIL OBERHELMAN

For some, the quintessential heartbeat
of New Orleans lies in the
fine thin notes of an old jazz melody.
Others find it in the perfect fried oyster po-boy.
Still others see the city's soul
in the flashing neon lights of a Carnival
megafloat as it rolls past clamoring crowds.
Me, I always wanted to live in a camelback shotgun.

Renée Peck
Home and Garden editor
The Times-Picayune

Home of 1920's Jazz Cornetist Johnny DeDroit, Camp St.,
Uptown, by Mary Fitzpatrick

Eastlake Camelback 1984, © Jeffrey Lamb 2007

Twins, by Joseph Carl Kerkman
Stripped to the Bones, Holy Cross, by Amelie LeBreton

Living Quarters
(A Shot Gun House)

Did you live in a shot gun house?

The living room in front of
A bedroom

A bedroom in front of
A bathroom

A bathroom in front of
A bedroom

No hall sometimes at all

Then
The kitchen
And a back porch

One straight line

Sit
Sleep
Bathe
And dine
Ours, yours, theirs and mine

Behind
The front porch

Darrlyn A. Smith,
The New Orleans 7th Ward Nostalgia Dictionary,
by permission of Joseph Smith
neworleans7thward.com

Shotguns are to New Orleans what brownstones are to New York, rowhouses to Philadelphia, single houses to Charleston and bungalows to Chicago. A unique and truly sustainable design, the building techniques are traditional, and the materials are local and hearty. They house families in close proximity, they are right for the climate, and there are lots of them.

William G. Barry, Jr. AIA, LEED

Barracks St., French Quarter, ©Louis Sahuc/ Photo Works
Georgetown Rowhouse, by Mary Fitzpatrick
Charleston Single House, by Sellers Grantham

2309 First Street cannot be definitively called the birthplace of jazz, but it can almost certainly be pinpointed as the location where the first man of jazz grew up. There was no jazz or ragtime band recalled by anyone before Buddy Bolden put his band together.

Donald M. Marquis, jazz curator emeritus, Louisiana State Museum, and author of *In Search of Buddy Bolden: First Man of Jazz*

In the spring of 1958
on the sun porch
of his Milan Street shotgun,
Walker Percy began to work on a novel.
He was 42 years old.
The Moviegoer won the
National Book Award in 1962.

***Edwin Blair,* "Literary Habitats,"**
***Preservation in Print,* April 1995**

Jazzman Buddy Bolden's Home 2000, Central City, by Mary Fitzpatrick
Author Walker Percy's Home, Uptown, by Alex Lemann

Her wide pine hips know the shape of
waiting beneath swirling brackets,
For the slow waltz of summer as it creeps and
sinks against her partial white fence...

Rebecca Rebouche, poet

Pauline, ©Frank Relle Photography

For sale sign in my dreams: White Single Shotgun on Touro Street. Bought, Sold, Rented, Renovated and Neglected No Less than 24 Times by All Manner of Occupants, Including Three Short-order Cooks, Two Rail Workers, Horse Jockey with Career Losing Record (0-1), Single Mother Managing the Best She Could, Roughneck (Two Weeks On, Two Weeks Off), Young Couple on the Outs, Resident Dermatologist, Old Couple that Knew a Thing or Two About Letting Things Slide, and Most Recently, Auto Mechanic Who Enjoyed Sitting on the Front Porch in a Spare 1985 Chevette Passenger Seat. Currently Vacant but Hanging on for Dear Life.

Patrick Strange, **writer**

Prieur, ©Frank Relle Photography

I think of shotguns as the backbones of New Orleans.

Sometimes they look almost like vertebrae lined up on the street,

but it is the people who live in them who really support and sustain the city.

Camille Strachan, attorney and board chair of National Trust Community Development Financial Institution, Inc.-
a non-profit subsidiary of the National Trust for Historic Preservation

Annie, Lower Garden District, by Beverly Lamb
Gentilly Sno-Balls 2004, by Mary Fitzpatrick
Uptown, ©Louis Sahuc/Photo Works
Achille and Bill, by Averil Oberhelman
My Favorite Shotgun, by Deborah Burst
Camelback and Cab, by Sara Orton
Shotgun on Bayou St. John, Esplanade Ridge, by Alysha Jordan

a brief history

Peace in a Time of
War, © Craig Morse

The shotgun house has a tangled and somewhat murky history. No one person invented the shotgun house, and in writing about its origins, historians have presented an array of competing theories, none of which can be definitively proved or disproved. What is known for certain is that the shotgun house as we know it today – a long, skinny, raised, free-standing rectangle composed of a series of rooms lined up behind each other – first emerged in New Orleans in the 1830s. Over the next half century, the shotgun became one of the most frequently used house types in New Orleans and a common sight all over the South.

The Creole cottage can be distinguished from the shotgun by its roof line, which runs parallel to the street. Some have argued that the shotgun evolved out of the Creole cottage. Photo by Alex Lemann.

New Orleans' role as the incubator of the shotgun has given rise to the sup-

The earliest shotguns were typically built right up against the sidewalk, with no porch and a shallow roof overhang. Photo by Mary Fitzpatrick.

position that the shotgun was invented in New Orleans. In support of this idea, many have pointed out the practice of dividing land along the Mississippi into long, thin plots with short frontages on the river, perhaps giving rise to long, thin houses. There is also a theory that property tax in New Orleans was calculated based on the frontage width of a house, thus the need for a long, skinny house.

According to former New Orleans notarial archivist Sally K. Reeves, however, there is no evidence that houses were ever taxed by the front foot, nor are shotguns necessarily narrower than the earlier Creole cottage, just deeper. The shotgun's popularity in urban areas may have more to do with the fact that it simply allows more living space to be crammed into a block.

It also has been pointed out that the shotgun house is not an exclusively urban

phenomenon; the first shotgun may have been built in a rural area,

and shotguns are still a common sight in the countryside.

One competing theory of the shotgun's origins, advanced most

prominently by John Michael Vlach, is based on the idea that it may

have been imported to New Orleans from Haiti. According to this

theory, the rise of the shotgun house in the 1830s corresponded to a

The Eastlake style, popular from around 1880 to 1905, is famous for its intricate millwork. Photo by Mary Fitzpatrick.

dramatic increase in the black population over the same period, as immigrants from

Haiti came to the city. Other scholars, however, including Reeves, suggest that the

shotgun actually evolved out of the Creole cottage, as craftsmen worked to adapt it

to New Orleans lots.

The fact remains that the shotgun is one of the simplest possible house types, being just a series of rooms, and it is hard to show that it derives from one single source. Ultimately, the shotgun house has the basic advantages of being compact and well suited to the heat, making it an excellent choice for New Orleans and other Southern cities, where it was developed and redeveloped in new ways.

Developing out of the Greek Revival style in the mid 19th century, the Italianate style was inspired by Italian Renaissance architecture and was introduced to America by way of England. Photo by Alex Lemann.

The earliest shotguns were typically built right up against the sidewalk, with a hipped or gabled roof on the front and a shallow roof overhang. Later, they retreated from the street and began to feature a porch and a more substantial roof overhang, often supported by elaborate brackets. Variations on the simple plan also were improvised, including the double shotgun and the camelback. Greek Revival shotguns were built with stately columns and classical details, and Eastlake shotguns were styled with decorative mill-work so intricate as to be almost fanciful. Later shotguns even have Arts and Crafts details or look like California bungalows.

Side galleries were sometimes enclosed to form interior hall-ways. Photo by Jeffrey Lamb.

After going through many stylistic permutations, the shotgun fell out of fashion in the first quarter of the 20th century. Air conditioning made its natural ventilation irrelevant, and the automobile made houses squeezed up against each other without driveways inconvenient. The mid-century neighborhoods of New Orleans, with their slab-on-grade ranch houses, had no place for the shotgun.

With the increasing appreciation of historic architecture in the late 20th century, the shotgun house enjoyed something of a renaissance. Today, shotguns are recognized as treasures of American architecture, well worth preserving. There is a sense that the shotgun house has contributed something special to the urban and social fabric of New Orleans, and both its legacy and survival are now major priorities.

Alex Lemann

o u r   s t o r i e s

ADRIENNE PETROSINI

It was the mid-1970s. The word on the street was that Mr. M. lived in one half of the corner double and his wife lived in the other. No one knew if they were married or divorced. My young heart couldn't understand their relationship. Every afternoon Mr. M. would leave his side of the double, stop, greet my daughter and give her a stick of gum. We never saw Mrs. M. Today, two marriages later, I am sure Mr. and Mrs. M. had the ideal living arrangement.

Adrienne Petrosini,
Clinical Social Worker

Divided Lives, Carrollton, by Amy Loewy

In the mid '80s my identical twin Foster moved into a shotgun, identical to ours, two houses down the block. Carmen and I had been married a short time, but Foster was still quite the rake about town and had left some broken hearts in his wake. Based on inside information, our friend from childhood, Billy Freiberg, warned me that when I went outside each morning to pick up the newspaper, I should consider wearing bulletproof attire in case one of the disgruntled young women got confused as to which identical shotgun belonged to which identical twin and took her displeasure with Foster out on me!

Kelly Duncan, **attorney**

French Quarter, © Charles Leche

James Nolan, Esplanade Ridge, courtesy James Nolan
James Nolan Revisiting Mémère's Shotgun, 2007, by Alex Lemann
James Nolan's Family Christmas in Shotgun Parlor, courtesy James Nolan
Mémère's Frigidaire and Family, courtesy James Nolan

In those days nobody called it child care, just Mémère's. When I was a boy and underfoot in the kitchen, my great-aunt Marguerite would say, "Go to the front gallery and see if you're there." I'd run through the dining room with the new Frigidaire, down the hall between the bathroom and side gallery (where the ice man used to come), through my great-grandmother's bedroom where the rosary droned on the radio, through my great-aunt's bedroom with a crucifix over the single bed, through my grandparents' bedroom where Pépère was taking a nap, through my teenage aunt's bedroom where she was listening to Elvis, through the parlor's pocket doors, and then swing open the creaky screen door onto the porch with its weathered rockers. "Quick, come see," I'd shout from the front to the back of the shotgun house, "I'm there."

James Nolan, **writer**

I was so scared of ghosts when I was little. One night I was sleeping over at a new friend's shotgun house, and I called my dad crying that I wanted to come home because of the whole ghost thing. He asked me to go to the front door and let him know if I could look all the way through the house and see the back door. When I said yes, my dad told me that I had absolutely nothing to worry about – if a ghost came in the front door he would be pulled right through and out the back before he could cause any trouble.

Shelby Westfeldt, coffee importer

No Place for Ghosts, Holy Cross, by Mary Fitzpatrick

I put a cross on the front door and back door and all the windows to keep the ghosts out. The good spirits, they will leave when they see the crosses, but for the bad spirits I pour alcohol (whiskey is good) across the front door steps or leave a few cigarettes and they never come in because they got what they came for.

Brother Charles Banks, carpenter

Holy Cross Home of Brother Charles, by Averil Oberhelman

We didn't have a living room except at Christmas when we'd put the couch and a tree in the front room. Most of the time it was my bedroom. I'd sleep right inside the screen doors facing Magazine Street and listen to the people walk up and down the sidewalk. The way I was raised, when I got up in the morning and got dressed then I was never allowed back in my bedroom until it was time to go to bed. My mother cleaned the whole house every day and when she finished a room she closed the door. She even waxed the ivy plant on her hope chest. My grandmother did all the cooking and made our clothes. Mother starched the clothes, but we took our ironing to a woman, even the sheets on the bed. And we always had red beans on Monday.

Anthony Probst, contractor and retired fishing camp manager

Mondays, ©Louis Sahuc/Photo Works

40

Bowen's Camp St. home ..1948

Donald   Burt   John Jr.

My uncle and aunt bought a shotgun at 5432-34 Camp Street in 1925 for $7,800 and raised four children in one side of the double. My mother, dad, grandfather and I moved into the other side in 1943. The street was paved with clam shells covered in an oily tar mix, and the open garbage wagon was drawn by two mules. The Roman Candy Man lived just a few blocks away on Constance Street where he had a stable next door for his horse, the ice man delivered to the house and vendors for most anything came by on foot and in wagons. The double was sold in 2005 for $453,000 and converted into a single. I still go back to the old neighborhood from time to time.

Albert Easterling, Jr., **retired fidelity and surety bond underwriter and wholesale battery salesman**

The Bowen Brothers on Porch of 5434 Camp Street in 1948, Uptown, courtesy Albert Easterling, Jr.

A peculiar sound emanates from my shotgun each evening. Walking along the brick path to my rear entrance, I hear it. Da-Da-Da-Da-Da-Da. The thunderous sound moves in a straight line, unimpeded by interior walls. It is the result of sixteen feline feet, galloping in a kind of kitty derby, from the starting post at my cypress front door, through the bedroom stretch and ending at the finish line at the back door. The tails of my four cats wind around my ankles as I enter. In last place in the race is my dog, Birch, his claws click-clicking lightly on the heart pine floor. He drops his ball at my feet as if to remind me a shotgun is well designed for a game of fetch, too.

Celeste Stover, **animal lover, writer**

Bob Zmuda, Founder of Comic Relief, Greets Jeff, Holy Cross, by Mary Fitzpatrick

The double shotgun on Aline Street is the story of our family. My great-grandfather Louis Weber delivered milk to this neighborhood by horse-drawn cart. My grandfather Edward quit school after third grade to deliver newspapers. With their combined incomes, my frugal German great-grandmother (Josephine Fuchs Weber) set aside enough money to build their shotgun double. When it was completed in the early 1920s, she moved into half and my grandfather and his new family moved into the other side. They had coal burning fireplaces, an outhouse and one closet on each side.

Dianne Weber, landscape architect, grounds department head at Audubon Nature Institute

The Weber House, Uptown, by Dianne Weber

Privacy in a shotgun?

I had more privacy in the United States Air Force.

Try tiptoeing through the parlor,

the dining room, the kitchen and

your parent's bedroom after curfew!

Forrest M. Ricks Jr.,
building technician, retired air force inspector

Forrest Ricks Sr. and Friend, 1975, Tremé, courtesy Forrest Ricks Jr.

My Newman High School notebooks were covered in sketches and doodles of my favorite shotguns. Years later, one of my best high school friends was living in a great shotgun Uptown and hosted a wild engagement party where the B-52's hit "Love Shack" was played incessantly while guests danced on counter tops, chairs and anything that would support us. Now, a good decade later, when I see that particular classic shotgun style house, I refer to it as The Love Shack rather than a mere shotgun. I cherish the fact so many remain.

Bryan Batt, designer, owner of Hazelnut Shop, actor, a.k.a. Salvatore Romano on AMC's *Mad Men*

5265 Laurel Street, Uptown, ©Jeff Pounds Photography

...my father telephoned Emmay Waldman to tell her the other side of our house was for rent. Mrs. Waldman was a retired real-estate broker who acted as a liaison between uptown New Orleans' well-connected prospective tenants and landlords. For a reasonable commission and psychological satisfaction, she would consult her waiting list and place wild-streak bachelors with long suffering widows; insolvent divorcees with gallant old attorneys ("Now don't concern yourself about paying exactly on the minute dear. This rental property is chiefly a tax shelter."); child-blessed women with landladies who had wall-scribbling broods of their own.

Sheila Bosworth, writer, from ***Almost Innocent***

Waiting for Colin, French Quarter, by Alex Lemann

I tell my friend I'll take a picture of the shotgun she rented for 35 years. I have good intentions. She's 82 now, in Phoenix, in assisted living, still wanting to come back. Still wanting to know what's happening. But the house she rented hasn't been touched since the storm, when her life savings floated up from under her bed and in her mattress, lapped against walls and doors and windows and the sewing machine that had been her mother's. I carry with me a stamped envelope addressed to her, ready for the photograph I can't bring myself to take.

Karen Laborde, **writer and artist**

Moon Over Shotgun, by Stephanie K. Hierholzer

At one point there were
so many McIlhennys
living in the block of shotguns
on Coliseum Street
that neighbors called it
Tabasco® Row.

Paul McIlhenny,
**CEO and president of
McIlhenny Company,
makers of Tabasco® sauce**

Hall's Row designed by Henry Howard in 1867, Coliseum St. between Philip and First, Garden District,
© 2003 Robert S. and Jan White Brantley

Yellow Vine in Gert Town, by Carol Dotson

What is this thing covering me
that started as a wispy little
vine spread over the back door.
I really don't care. I was caught
up watching the faces slowly
fade from the neighborhood.
Late one afternoon I was boarded
up, and then I noticed it, this
mass of foliage. Today I wear it
as my Easter bonnet, buttery
yellow flowers and curls of vine
ribbon dangling from my roof.
Over time it just might become
my casket spray.

Patrice Joan Boyd

I fell in love with a little shotgun double in Mid-City. It had a single floor to ceiling window, wooden Venetian blinds, pocket doors and closed up coal-burning fireplaces with mantles in every room except the kitchen. Never mind that a marble placed at the front door would roll right out the back. Shotgun house with a tilt, you know. I later joked with my friends that I got fat living in that house because it was downhill to the kitchen and so hard to get back once you were there.

Cedelas Hall, writer, program director for medical rehabilitation unit

Shotgun 2, Mid-City, by Emily Gula
Bywater, ©J. Stirling Barrett

public spaces

MARY FITZPATRICK

At a time when American cities have been lost in a tangle of suburbs or given themselves over to high-rises, New Orleans has maintained a distinctive urban life. The density created by those old French surveyors assured that people would interact with one another, as did the front porches and stoops built directly on the sidewalk. Is it any wonder that such neighborhoods have proved so fertile for what might be called the social arts? There are many reasons why New Orleanians have long excelled in cooking, music-making, dancing and story-telling. The interaction of diverse cultures fostered by shotgun houses is certainly a major one.

S. Frederick Starr, **author and member of**
Louisiana Repertory Jazz Ensemble

Sunday Social Arts in Tremé, 2006, series by Mary Fitzpatrick

On our daily walks my husband Esmond and I go past a row of gingerbread shotguns. An elderly lady used to sit on her porch and never miss calling a sweet "hello" to Esmond. On one early morning walk we discovered she had fallen while getting her newspaper. Esmond helped her up and back to her rocker on the porch. She died a few weeks later. We learned then that her neighbors along the row had a reverse mortgage on her shotgun so that she could spend her last days rocking and greeting the handsome men walking by.

Margo Phelps

Walking and Rocking on Eighth Street, Garden District, by Mary Fitzpatrick

When I was little I wasn't allowed to walk across the street to my best friend Bitsy Bourgeois's house without an adult. So Bitsy and I would wait impatiently on our front porches for the mailman. He would drop off the letters and then lead me across the street to play with my friend.

Brandi Couvillion

Don't You Leave This Porch, New Marigny,
by Averil Oberhelman

They used to say, "I'm from the Nine and I don't mind dyin'" because the neighborhood was so tough. But to me it was just a beautiful place. My mother raised me and my three brothers in half of her aunt's double shotgun in the Lower Ninth Ward. Everyday I had to go outside and wash the sidewalk because when the chores were done we'd all sit on the stoop and talk to the neighbors. There was always something happening. Fats Domino used to frequent a bar on my street. He would pull up in a black Cadillac. Word would get around that Fats was setting up the bar, and we'd all run down to Nick's where Fats would buy drinks for the adults and candy for the kids.

Janie Blackmon, **financial consultant**

St. Thomas, Irish Channel, ©Katherine Slingluff
The Stoop, French Quarter 1984, ©Jeffrey Lamb
2007

In the 1200 block of St. Claude Street in Tremé the stoops and banquettes of shotgun houses have once again become the meeting place for Katrina-displaced family and friends who have found themselves back in this old neighborhood, door poppin', stoop sittin' and getting re-acquainted with the close relationships that rows of shotgun houses bring.

Naydja Bynum
doctor of nursing administration and
Tremé community activist

Stoop Sittin' and Door Poppin', Tremé, by Naydja Bynum

Dodie and Lillian Powers, Uptown, by Beverly Lamb

We didn't have camp or summer vacations; we had the front porch. We played jacks, pick-up-sticks, and Old Maid card games. My brother read a lot of comic books in the wicker rocking chair. Curiously, there was a man who came around with a little pull cart full of second-hand comic books, and his livelihood depended on the small fees he exacted for exchanging comic books with those already read.

Janice Grijns,
**remembering a childhood
in Bywater**

I stumbled out of the house at 6:45 a.m. on Mardi Gras morning. Costumed and hung over from Lundi Gras, I did not know if I had the energy to make it through the Zulu parade – until I heard the boom of a base drum as I rounded the corner of Toledano and Magazine, followed by the wild blasts of a brass band. I noticed that I was the only spectator for this small early morning parade and followed it all the way up to Amelia Street. I could tell that everyone in the parade was as tired as I was, but on Mardi Gras that doesn't matter.

Stephen Houser, photographer

Second Line 7 A.M. Magazine Street, Uptown, by Stephen Houser

When I was little my uncle Stephen lived in a shotgun cottage at the foot of Broadway and River Road. He was a dashing bachelor and had a Dalmatian named Gus that went everywhere with him, and he had actual shotguns to go with the cottage for he went hunting a lot. It seemed quaint and somehow racy or daring or debonair to have an uncle who was a bachelor in his thirties; but then he got married and my brother and I sang at his wedding and when his father died, he moved out of the shotgun cottage and back into the house he was born in. So his household then became more elaborate and his daring debonair days in the shotgun cottage were over.

Nancy Lemann, **author**

Raised Shotgun, by Joseph Carl Kerkman

My son moved to New Orleans from Naples, Italy, where we're from, and I visited him at his shotgun house by Magazine Street. My son went to work. I cleaned his house, washed his clothes, cooked his dinner, and then sat on his front porch, just like Naples. I'd be on that porch for two minutes and something would happen. I never wanted to go inside, just like Naples. One year my son bought a brand new house far away from Magazine. Mama, you'll love the mall, he said. Where's the front porch, I asked. Mama, I have a patio all to myself! When he left for work I pulled a chair out to the front yard and sat there waiting for something to happen. Mama, the neighbors will think you're crazy, go sit on the patio, my son said. Front yard, patio, it didn't matter. Nothing ever happened.

Andrea Franco

Stoop Sitting in the Irish Channel, by Mark Sindler
It's a Red Day, Irish Channel, by Averil Oberhelman
Zero, Faubourg Marigny, by Kevin Barnes

Neutral Ground, New Marigny, by Averil Oberhelman
Checkers, ©Christopher Porché West
Seventh Ward Soldier, ©Christopher Porché West

p u b l i c   a r t

MARY FITZPATRICK

In their simple and repetitive form, shotguns provide the framework for a dazzling kaleidoscope of self-expression. A shotgun façade is a blank page, just waiting to be filled.

Alex Lemann

Won't You Come In?, Uptown, by Mary Fitzpatrick
His & Hers Barber Shop, by Mark Sindler

Red, White, Black and Blue, Bywater, by David Fields
The Tile Setter's House, Bywater, ©Carolyn Long

When I first moved into the old Two Sister's restaurant in Bywater, people were always stopping by to look. Tourists on rented scooters, neighborhood drunks who saw the Falstaff sign proclaiming six beers for a $1.20. For a while, my roommate and I considered setting up shop and making some side cash, but visitors started to dwindle when the landlord's added signage got political. The visitors we get now are mostly local radicals who pull up on their bicycles, point, and say things like, "I hear they're organizing in that house." We shoo them off same as we do the drunks. We politely say, "You don't know anything about what's going on in here."

Case Miller
Construction Manager

Two Sisters and Plato the Cat, Bywater, by Adrienne Petrosini

1306 Music Street belongs to Arthur Smith, an elderly folk artist. He is known for decorating the St. Louis Cemetery No. 1 wall vault of his grandmother, Amanda Boswell Carroll, with hand-colored and collaged photocopied portraits, as well as his mother's grave in Carrollton Cemetery and a grave for the "unknown dead" in Holt Cemetery. LeMieux Gallery had an exhibition of his work. His shotgun house, pictured in 1997, had no running water or electricity and was filled with plastic bags of trash. Mr. Smith lived on the street and earned a living by salvaging aluminum cans.

Carolyn Long, **author, retired conservator and current research associate at Smithsonian Institute**

Arthur's House, New Marigny, ©Carolyn Long

A shotgun seems to soak up a little bit of your soul,

and if someone tries to take it away… watch out!

Jackie Derks

U Loot U Dead, Bywater, by Mary Fitzpatrick
I'm Staying Put, Holy Cross, by Mary Fitzpatrick

Faith, by Leslie Parr
Heart House, by Stephanie K. Hierholzer

Neighborhood Watch, Carrollton, by Averil Oberhelman

Against contagious diseases and epidemics,

pray for us.

Against lightning and tempest,

pray for us.

Against destruction by flood,

pray for us.

**Intercession to
Our Lady of Prompt Succor,
repeated often in New Orleans**

Visual candy
Like Grandma's
butter mints
Sweetly refreshing...

Amy Loewy, bookseller

Butter Mints, Uptown, by Amy Loewy
Jefferson Avenue, Uptown, by Beverly Lamb
Sui Generis, Uptown, by Sherry Lee Alexander
Lloyd and Gene's Block, Faubourg Marigny, by Mary Fitzpatrick

close ups

MARY FITZPATRICK

My family moved to New Orleans after the storm so that I could restart a small Presbyterian church. Finding our shotgun double to purchase made a difficult transition much sweeter. We love it for its Eastlake Victorian details (quoins on the sides, dramatic little iron fence, 12-foot ceilings, eight ornate cypress mantels), for its history (built in 1902 by a German streetcar conductor and among its eleven owners was Johnny Dedroit, a jazz pioneer), and most of all for where it sits – on the corner of Magazine and Henry Clay, a hub of the Uptown neighborhood where we can savor the people of New Orleans.

Raymond Cannata, minister

My House, Uptown, by Raymond Cannata

I remember how proud my friend Mary was when her antique twist doorbell arrived. After all of the repairs she made since the brackish waters flooded her home, this was a final feature that made it seem more complete. The stained glass inset offers a flash of color and a motif bordering each fireplace inside. I love the way the ridges of each section are thick and wavy yet still have reflection. So many diminutive patterns make up such a lovely door.

Charlotte Klasson, **freelance writer, editor and photographer**

Street Corner, French Quarter, ©Jeffrey Lamb 2007

Quoin:
A block that accentuates the corner of a building. In the case of the New Orleans shotgun, quoins are the vertical rows of wooden squares found on the edges of the façade.

Bracket:
The factory-produced, catalog-ordered architectural details that often adorn New Orleans shotguns achieved the pinnacle of their development in the bracket, the elaborately carved elements that supported the overhanging roof of the gallery.

Brackets, French Quarter, © Charles Leche

Shutters:

Working louvered shutters

are another of

the shotgun's many defenses

against heat.

Deb, Uptown, by Adrienne Petrosini

Gable:
The shotgun's roof ridge often terminated in a gable, a little triangular patch of wall that in some cases formed yet another canvas for ornamentation.

Gable, New Marigny, by Averil Oberhelman

Drop siding:

Wooden weatherboard with

an indentation at the top of each slat.

This allows the slats to fit together and

lie flat against each other.

In most cases, drop siding adorns

only the façade of a shotgun,

while the other walls are

covered with standard siding.

Shadows in the Marigny, ©Louis Sahuc/Photo Works

private spaces

ALEX LEMANN

Like anything so ubiquitous, shotguns are easy to take for granted and like the city itself, have shortcomings somehow more memorable than their assets. Speaking of assets, malleability is at the top of my list. Raised off the ground with empty attics and hollow walls, every conceivable modern advancement, from indoor plumbing to electrical conduit to air conditioning vents to speaker wire, had a place to be crammed without unduly disrupting the décor. Shotguns survived because they were adaptable, malleable, and were common, which is to say they weren't overly precious — the sort of rare creation with which tampering would be considered inappropriate, or even tragic. The ways in which shotgun residences have been lived in and modified are as diverse and creative as New Orleans itself.

Richard Sexton, **photographer, author and shotgun resident**

Marcus Fraser Interior, Bywater, from the book *New Orleans: Elegance and Decadence,* courtesy of Richard Sexton ©1993
Steven Hale Interior, Esplanade Ridge, courtesy of Richard Sexton ©1999

I thought to myself, that old shack would make a lovely home. My friends called me a fool, a genius and everything in between. Other than the typical challenges, the project was very smooth. To maximize space, the eaves are filled with mechanicals and storage. We combined old cypress fence rails with heavy-duty wire and turn-buckles to create an economical balcony railing for the attic room. It also makes the industrial connection with the bridge and interstate which are almost in my back-yard. Utility, function, energy – that old shack now has it all.

Sam Bridges, naturopathic doctor

Sam Bridges Interiors, Warehouse District, by Alex Lemann

Some people are narrow minded about shotgun houses — they think they're too small and don't have enough privacy. But there are easy solutions, tricks you can do! I created the illusion of space — double parlors that suggest a ballroom, French doors that expand the space out onto the porch and into my wild garden. One space flows to the next to make a stage set where real life takes place.

Mario Villa, designer

Mario Villa Interior, Esplanade Ridge, from the book
New Orleans: Elegance and Decadence, courtesy of
Richard Sexton ©1993

Hall's Row Interiors (Pio Lyons, renovation architect), Coliseum St. between First and Philip Streets, Garden District, ©2003 Robert S. and Jan White Brantley

A narrow shotgun lot requires a certain sort of garden. We decided to turn our outdoor habitat into a pond with intimate environments for meditation. Sometimes I sit right next to the house and sometimes I like to go to the end of the garden where the sound and mist from the waterfall bring me inner peace.

Andrea Foster

Andrea and Kelly's Garden, Irish Channel, by Kelly Nezat

We stay in one side of a beautiful yellow double shotgun home in Algiers Point. We are both from Durban, South Africa, and shotguns are a style that neither of us had encountered previously. We have spent this year living in London, then Brazil and now New Orleans. When we arrived and saw our home, we were amazed at the detail and how chic it was. The wooden floors, stone counter tops and high ceilings give a warm homey feel, which we love. It's the best place we've lived all year.

Clair-Louise Mead

Clair at Home in Algiers Point Thanks to Bobby and Kristin Gisleson-Palmer, by Hugo Morgado

I'm especially proud that our cottage is custom-designed for the historic neighborhood it's going in. This adaptation of a traditional shotgun home has tall windows and ceilings, doors with transoms, covered porches, operable shutters and a raised foundation. New construction, done right, can have a sense of history and still be built for busy 21st-century lifestyles.

Eleanor Griffin
Cottage Living editor-in-chief

Scenes from *Cottage Living* 2007 Idea Home (Eric Moser, Beaufort, S.C. architect; Holden & Dupuy Interior Design; partnership with PRC Modular Home, LLC, New Orleans Tourism and Marketing Corp. and Preservation Resource Center), 4505 Camp St., Uptown, Reprinted with permission of *Cottage Living* magazine. Parlor by Roger Foley. Kitchen and Living Room by Robbie Caponetto.

r e c y c l i n g

CAMILLE LOPEZ

101

3900 Annunciation Street, Uptown

On the Move to 3900 Annunciation St., Uptown, by Nairne Frazar
After Preservation Resource Center Renovation, by Operation Comeback

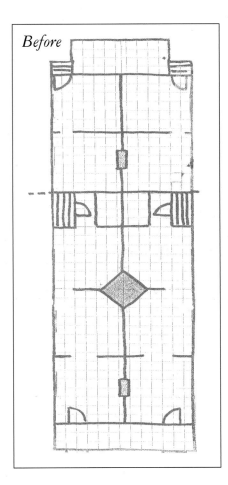

Before

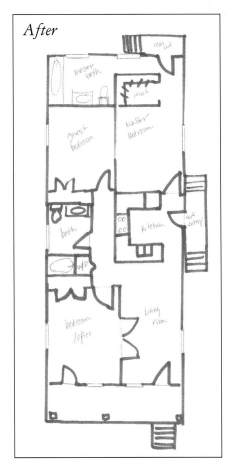

After

Renovation strategy: Converted to a single with two bedrooms and two baths, plus a flex room, which can be a third bedroom or office. Left one side entry for access to big side yard and parking. Moved other side entry door to rear to provide private yard access from master bedroom. Connected main living space to flex room with double doors that can stay open or closed for privacy.

PRC's Operation Comeback

625 General Taylor Street, Uptown

Before, 625 General Taylor St., Uptown, by Operation Comeback
After PRC Renovation, by Alex Lemann

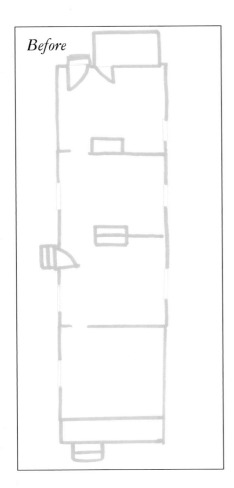

Before

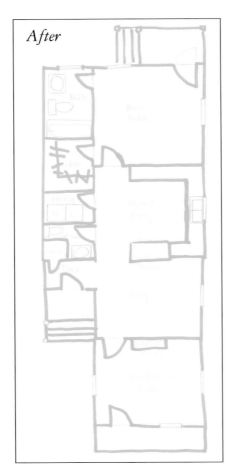

After

Renovation strategy: Added onto the side but maintained the off-street parking. Moved the entry to the side so the front room can be used either as a bedroom or a study. Made the most of the shallow lot by installing a deck off the master bedroom for private outdoor space. Added a side addition for baths, laundry and closet.

PRC's Operation Comeback

Studies show that $1 million spent

to rehab an older building creates

more jobs than the same amount

spent on new construction.

What's more, most of the

money spent on rehab stays in the region,

while most of the money spent on

new construction flies off to someplace else.

**_Richard Moe,_ president
National Trust for Historic Preservation**

Slated for Demolition but Renovated by Felicity Street Redevelopment Project,
1134 Baronne St., Central City,
Before courtesy FSRP and After by Averil Oberhelman

I stressed to Congress

that we have to preserve what we have.

And we have to train young people

because this is going to go on for years.

Earl Barthe, 5th generation New Orleans plasterer and National Heritage Fellow, speaking after Hurricane Katrina

Former Home of Legendary Jazzman Edward "Kid" Ory Renovated by Preservation Resource Center in 2002 (assisted by students with New Orleans Crafts Guild), 2133 Jackson Ave., Central City, Before by PRC's Operation Comeback and After by Mary Fitzpatrick

Let's say that we tear down – instead of rehabilitate – one small building, about 25 feet wide and 100 feet deep.

We have now wiped out the entire environmental benefit

from the last 1,344,000 Coke cans that were recycled, in terms of landfill.

Donovan Rypkema, economist

Renovated After Katrina by Joel Dondis and Laura Gordon, 2332 Laurel St., Irish Channel, Before courtesy Historic District Landmarks Commission and After by Alex Lemann

We can cheer when we turn
used tires into asphalt shingles and
recycle newspapers into fiberboard.
But when we reuse a historic building,
we're recycling the whole thing.

Donovan Rypkema, economist

Slated for Demolition — Moved from Original Site by Preservation Resource Center — Renovated in 1999 by Parkway Partners, 1137 Baronne St., Central City, Before and After by Mary Fitzpatrick

Rehabilitation construction uses 23% less energy
than new construction, primarily
because the work is more labor intensive
than material intensive,
depleting fewer natural resources.

**Office of Archaeology and Historic Preservation,
Department of the Interior**

Katrina Damaged Home Gutted and Under Renovation by PRC's
Rebuilding Together and National Trust for Historic Preservation (with support from Hearst Corp., Elderhostel, and RT National), 5209 Dauphine St.,
Holy Cross, Before by Mary Fitzpatrick and After by Alex Lemann

By turning two shotgun houses —

the city's most common type of residence and

therefore very familiar to children —

into a school and connecting them with a covered

porch, another typical New Orleans house feature,

the Trinity nursery school makes a brilliant

transition from home to school for the little children.

Mary Fitzpatrick
Preservation in Print, April 2004

Altered Façade Covers Future Trinity Nursery School,
Lower Garden District, Before courtesy of Trinity Episcopal School
(Waggonner & Ball, architects), After by Mary Fitzpatrick

If it can happen here, it can happen anywhere in the city. We targeted the most challenging block, converted a liability into an asset and, in doing so, attracted more than 200 private projects and $11 million to the neighborhood within a few years. Long-time homeowners who had watched the equity in their homes decline and their quality of life erode have new hope and confidence.

Meg Lousteau, former assistant director of PRC's Operation Comeback, on the renovation of eight houses in 600 block of General Taylor Street

Blighted 600 Block of General Taylor Street Renovated by Preservation Resource Center
(with support from Whitney National Bank), Uptown, Before by Operation Comeback and After by Mary Fitzpatrick

The greenest building is one that is already built.

5200 Block of Dauphine St., renovations by National Trust for Historic Preservation and PRC's Rebuilding Together (with support of Hearst Corp., Order of Malta and Louisiana Division of Historic Preservation Historic Building Grant), Before and After by Mary Fitzpatrick

Carl Elefante, **AIA, LEED, AP**
principal architect and director of Sustainable Design
Quinn|Evans Architects, Ann Arbor and Washington, D.C.

epilogue

© CHARLES LECHE

Years ago I was admiring a particular row of shotguns, and I began thinking about the civic virtue of these houses. Simple house type that it is, a shotgun, nevertheless, often presents an elaborate façade. Some historians attribute this to an effort to make a modest house look more imposing than it actually is. I think differently. I believe that this emphasis on the front façade, with its design excellence and friendly stoop or porch, reflects the owner's sense of neighborhood and community tradition. Whether identical to its neighbors or a complementary variation, each façade takes its place alongside other shotguns,

When I see a substantial Greek Revival shotgun single like this, built in 1860, it takes my breath away. Photo by Andrea Foster.

Creole cottages and larger homes sprinkled in the mix. The idea has always been to belong, to fit in, not to stand out – to contribute to the making of a remarkable streetscape with enduring appeal. The stylistic variety makes a strong statement about a rich tradition of collective pride and civic awareness.

The shotgun house has evolved through the decades to meet a wide range of housing needs, while still allowing individualism. It can be basic or expanded and adorned. In its flexibility, the shotgun reflects a civic capability to incorporate diverse residential needs with a holistic approach to urban planning. New Orleans is blessed with one of the best urban plans in the country. Originated early in the 18th century, this plan served the city well as it grew in the 19th century to be one of the three largest American cities. The shotgun house became a perfect vehicle for filling out New Orleans' unique and highly functional urban plan, regardless of neighborhood. Shotguns make up more than 64 percent of the historic downtown neighborhood Bywater and 52 percent of the Uptown National Register district at the opposite end of the city. The Garden District, with 1025 buildings, has 215 shotgun houses mixed in with 20 mansions. Shotgun houses are everywhere in our historic city.

When owners undertake ambitious restorations of deteriorated shotgun houses, they are doing more than saving an historic building and creating a dream home. They are contributing to the perpetuation of the unique quality of urban life in New Orleans, a quality of life that depends upon a commitment to design excellence and a civic consciousness and involvement on the part of all residents.

Patricia H. Gay
Preservation Resource Center Executive Director

The Preservation Resource Center of New Orleans
thanks the professional and amateur photographers
who donated the use of their images for this book

Sherry Lee Alexander

Kevin Barnes

J. Stirling Barrett
StirlingBarrett.com

John Bedford

Wendi Berman
strawberryblog.com

Robert S. and Jan White Brantley
brantleyphotography@cox.net

Deborah Burst

Naydja Bynum

Robert Cangelosi, Jr.

Raymond Cannata

Robbie Caponetto/
Cottage Living Magazine

Carol Dotson
cdot60@hotmail.com

Paul Douroux

Albert Easterling, Jr.

Felicity Street
Redevelopment Project

David Fields

Mary Fitzpatrick

Roger Foley/*Cottage Living* Magazine

Andrea Foster

Nairne Frazar

Sellers Grantham

Emily Gula

Stephanie K. Hierholzer

Historic District
Landmarks Commission
cityofno.com

Stephen Houser
Jshphoto.net

Alysha Jordan

Joseph Carl Kerkman
jckerkman@hotmail.com

Charlotte H. Klasson

Beverly Lamb

Jeffrey Lamb
jefflambphoto.com

Amelie LeBreton

Charles E. Leche
charleslechephotography.com

Alex Lemann

Carolyn Long

Camille Lopez

Amy Loewy

Hugo Morgado

Craig Morse
culturesubculture.com

Kelly Nezat

James Nolan

Averil Oberhelman

Sara Orton

Leslie Parr

Adrienne Petrosini
adrienne_pet@yahoo.com

Christopher Porché West
porche-west.com

Jeff Pounds Photography
jeffpounds.com

PRC Operation Comeback Staff

Frank Relle Photography
Frankrelle.com

Forrest M. Ricks, Jr.

Louis Sahuc/Photo Works
photoworksneworleans.com

Richard Sexton
richardsextonstudio.com

Mark Sindler

Katherine Slingluff
slingluffphoto.com

Trinity Episcopal School

Dianne Weber

Special thanks to New Orleans Tourism and Marketing Corporation and
to *Cottage Living* magazine and its photography department,
which juried the Preservation Resource Center exhibit
new orleans' favorite shotguns